Secrets of the Subterranean Cities

Secrets of the Subterranean Cities

Princess Sharula Aurora Dux
and Dianne Robbins

Dedication

In Tribute to Sharula — who risked her life to leave Telos, a Subterranean City beneath Mount Shasta, to bring to our surface population information about the Underground Cities.

Contents

Foreword

It is my privilege to publish this book on behalf of Sharula Aurora Dux, who still resides on Earth's surface, location unknown, to protect her identity.

The transcript of this book was taken from a cassette tape Sharula made in the late 1980s, that I transcribed and digitized and put on YouTube and my website for the enlightenment of the people of Earth. These are Sharula's own spoken words, and not a word was changed.

Traveling through the pages of this book will vibrationally connect you to Adama and the city of Telos, where you can learn how another civilization has gained its immortality and lives in peace and abundance just below the surface of our feet.

If this information were to be utilized by

all people and all our governments on the surface, it would change the trajectory our planet is currently taking from a planet veering towards destruction to reconstruction.

May you experience the possibilities and wonders that life offers through the pages of this book.

~ Dianne Robbins

Introduction

Currently, a few hundred brave sub-terraneans are working on the surface. In order to blend with the masses, they have undergone temporary cellular change so that, physically, they don't tower above the rest of us. They may be recognized by their gentle, sensitive nature and somewhat mysterious accent.

We wish to introduce you to Princess Sharula Aurora Dux, the daughter of the Ra and Rana Mu of Telos. Sharula has been officially appointed Ambassador to the surface world by the Agartha Network. She was born in 1725, and looks thirty. This book is courtesy of her firsthand experience. It contains the transcript of two tapes that Sharula recorded in the early 1990s, which can be heard at www. DianneRobbins.com/dux-audio.htm.

All planets are Hollow,
and are inhabited by human life
of one vibration or another.

The Sun is also Hollow,
and is not hot, but cold.

Our Earth is Hollow,
and contains an Inner Central Sun.

Atlantean-Lemurian Wars

Let me tell you a tale of two continents. One, in the Atlantic, called Atlantis. Another, in the Pacific, called Lemuria, or Mu for short. Twenty-five thousand years ago, these two continents were battling each other on the ideology of the day. Look at them as the two largest children on the block, and the two highest civilizations.

At that time they both had two different ideas about which direction civilization should go. The Lemurians felt that the other less-evolved cultures should be left alone to continue on their own evolution scale. The Atlanteans believed that all the less-evolved cultures should be brought under sway by the two evolved ones.

This caused a series of wars between Atlantis and Lemuria. In these series of wars thermonuclear devices were used, and when the wars were over and the dust cleared, in reality there was no winner. The Outback in Australia, the Mojave Desert, parts of the Gobi Desert, and the Sahara are all remains to remind man of the futility of this type of war.

During the wars themselves, people highly civilized stooped to quite low levels, but they, too, at the end, realized the futility of such behavior. Lemuria and Atlantis became the victims of their own aggressions. Both the Lemurian homeland and the Atlantean homeland had been weakened by the wars, thus they knew that in about 15,000 years, both of their continents were going to sink completely. The Atlanteans had their second set of cataclysms, which reduced Atlantis from a large continent to a series of islands. Lemuria, in essence, did somewhat of the same.

However, you might say, "Well, why would

the people be upset at that time for something that was going to happen 15,000 years in the future?" In those days, people lived for 20,000–30,000 years commonly. They understood that many of those who caused the havoc would see the end of the destruction.

Telos & Subterranean Cities

When Lemuria, which went down first, almost 200 years before Atlantis sank, they petitioned the Agartha Network. The Agartha Network is a network of subterranean cities that is guided by a city called Shamballa the Lesser (to distinguish it from Shamballa the Greater, which is the etheric Shamballa over the Gobi Desert). Shamballa the Lesser was created when the continent of Hyperborea was vacated after Earth lost her mantle[1] and the planet started receiving radioactive waves that they had not been victim to in the earlier times. So they started building subterranean cities over 100,000 years ago.

When Atlantis and Lemuria petitioned to build subterranean cities themselves and

---

1   See "Earth's Mantle" section, page 104.

to be accepted into the Agarthian Network, they had to prove to Shamballa the Lesser that they had learned the lessons of oppression, that they had learned the lessons of war. And they also had to prove it to many other agencies, such as the Confederation, which we will go into a little later. Atlantis and Lemuria had both been members of the Confederation, and when they started their war-like efforts against each other they were expelled temporarily from the Confederation and had to prove that they had also learned the lessons of peace to be allowed to be members of the Confederation again, to be accepted into it.

Mount Shasta is where the Lemurians chose to build their city. California was part of the colonies, part of the area of the Lemurian lands, and they understood that Mount Shasta and those areas of California would survive the cataclysms, Mount Shasta already being a place of great sacredness on this planet. They chose to reroute the lava tunnels from Shasta itself so that the volcano would not erupt again. And there was already a very large domed cavern within it, and they decided to build upon that, and they constructed the city that we now call Telos.

Telos was the name of the whole area of much of what is now the Southwest, and much of what is now California was originally called Telos, which meant "communication with spirit," "oneness with spirit," "understanding with spirit." It was constructed to hold a maximum of two million people.

When the cataclysms started, only 25,000 people were saved. Many had been brought to Telos before the cataclysms started, but when the second set started in Lemuria, the volcanoes started erupting so fast and sent so much debris into the air that, while they had intended to save at least a million people from the Lemurian mainlands, they were only able to save 25,000. Thus, that was what was left of the Lemurian culture, of the Lemurian mainland. Already the records had been brought from Lemuria to Telos. Already the temples had been built in Telos.

Earthquakes & Destruction

While Lemuria — or what was left of Lemuria, mainly Telos — was coping with the aftermath of the destruction of their continent, the earthquakes continued. During these earthquakes, the earth shook so hard, that in many, many places, it went right off of what you would now call the Richter scale.

When a continent sinks, the whole planet reacts. Earthquakes that reach the equivalent of what you would call a fifteen-point. These earthquakes were so intense that many people died from the sound of the earthquake, not from any effect of the quake itself, such as a building falling upon them or something. But a quake of that high of intensity created a screech through the atmosphere that killed many people simply from the sound of it.

In many other places the earthquakes were so intense that the earth was mostly clay. It liquified and acted like a sea of mud, swallowing whole cities — not just on the Lemurian mainland, but on many places on the planet. Another thing that came after that, as the continent itself went down, the tidal wave was so large that sometimes it went not just hundreds, but a thousand miles inland — the equivalent of a tidal wave starting on the coast of California and completely taking out Oklahoma City. Tidal waves like that were rampant, as well as the earthquakes. In some areas, the shaking never quit. It would be a constant swarm of if not large ones, then small quakes.

The Hierarchies, the Councils of this planet, understood this was going to happen. So they tried to construct both cities prior to the destruction of Lemuria itself, understanding that the Atlanteans would not get a lot of construction done under those circumstances. Also, at the same time, the great pyramid in Egypt was constructed, underneath the tutelage of the Lemurian high priest, better known as Thoth. And the Atlantean record chambers, which were geared to hold not only Atlantis' records, but Lemuria's, Pan's, Og's, Hyperborea . . . all of the other cultures that had existed and reached high levels upon this planet.

The Atlanteans moved into their city at just about the same time Lemuria sank, moving in first their priesthood, their greatest scientists, some of their greatest thinkers, to try to preserve their lives against the coming cataclysms. Atlantis itself started shaking at the same time Lemuria was going down, and Atlantis continued to shake and lose parts of its land for 200 years, before it, too, finally went completely down.

Surface Civilizations

For almost 2,000 years after the Atlantean and Lemurian catastrophes, the planet was still shaking. To lose two huge land masses within 200 years of each other, plus the planet was still witnessing the effects of the thermonuclear weapons that had been used in the Atlantean-Lemurian wars. Plus the fact that so much debris had been thrown into the atmosphere that it never became quite bright daylight for almost 300 years after Atlantis' destruction. This caused many, many life forms, plant forms, to go extinct. Plants that were common in Atlantean times, common in Lemurian times, that no longer exist, because they simply couldn't survive the long stages of filtered sunlight. Some have survived, yes, many animals and plants.

The human condition in those civilizations

that survived it . . . Egypt, Peru, Roma (better known as India), in many places people became so frightened by the constant earth activity that civilization, even in the last bastillions, started deteriorating very, very fast.

One question I have heard again and again is, "Well, if Atlantis and Lemuria existed, how come there is not more evidence on the surface of that?" Most of the cities were shook to rubble; that is why. Those that were not shaken to rubble were wiped out by the earthquakes or wiped out by the tidal waves. Even those who survived the tidal waves, the earthquakes . . . hunger was rampant . . . disease was rampant.

Some areas of civilization, like those future named Egypt and such, did survive. They kept their civilization intact, but even they started losing the highest elements of their civilization. Many, many machines quit working, because of the filtered sunlight.

Many, many people moved from the cities. They started feeling that living in the city was a deathtrap, because you never knew when a building was going to fall on you. What would look like a very strong building, have it go through 300 to 400 earthquakes . . . it's a goner.

Some buildings were built to withstand it. The great pyramid withstood the earthquakes, but it was built with sacred geometries. Other buildings like that throughout the planet survived, but most of the cities were completely reduced to rubble. In many areas they rebuilt the cities, but even then, each time the cities were rebuilt it was on a slightly less, should I say, technology. Each city was a little more primitive than the city before it.

The Atlanteans moved into their city which was built underneath the Mato Grasso plateau in what is now Brazil, which had been Atlantean territories at that time. Getting an understanding of what was happening on the surface, you can perhaps understand how the Lemurians or Atlanteans would prefer to be living underground.

Agartha Network

During this time, there was an integration, more and more, with the Agartha Network. As I explained earlier, Agartha is a Confederation of several subterranean cities. As a matter of fact, there are over 120 of them. Some of them were built in the very early times, such as Shamballa the Lesser, which is peopled with beings from Hyperborea. These are twelve-foot-tall beings.

Beings as man, on this planet, as on many other planets in this solar system, were originally of a height of about twelve feet. When we lost the mantle and started receiving more and more rays from the Sun to the planet that we were not used to coping with, it caused change within our bodies. Already, by the time Lemuria and Atlantis sank, man had gone from twelve feet to seven feet. Thus, the Atlanteans and Lemurians were around seven feet, and still are. And, as you can see, there has still been a lowering of the height on this planet. Thus, people have gone down to now, for the foremost, less than six feet. We have lost over a whole foot in just 10,000 years. However, that trend is starting to reverse itself, and as our spirituality is growing greater, we are slowly returning back to our original heights on this planet.

Within the Agartha Network, the cities that are allowed to join are only those that are based on light principles, only those that are based on love, only those that do not hurt, only those that are based on non-aggression. Within the Agarthian Network, — besides Telos, which is the capital, — there are four more cities, for instance, that are based on Lemurian technology and Lemurian ideas. One is called Rama, which is underneath India (Rama being the original name of India). Rama culture consisted of people that were almost pure Lemurian, before the so-called Aryan race entered India.

The other two cities that hold an allegiance to Telos, but are very independent, are Uighur cities. One is called Shonshe, which is under Tibet, not too far from the capital of Tibet. It is being sheltered from the surface by a Tibetan Lamasery. This is a Uighur city. Uighurs are a group of people that left Lemuria forty to fifty thousand years ago and situated themselves throughout much of what is Asia, India, and central Europe.

The second Uighur city is called Shingwa. Shingwa is in the Gobi, or should I say, under the Gobi Desert. This too is a Uighur city.

On top of the Atlantean city which is called Posid, that went underneath the Mato Grosso plateau, there is also another

Atlantean city. Just a little farther north there is another Atlantean city that is underneath the Atlantic Ocean, and several other smaller satellite cities throughout the planet.

As I said, these are all a member of the Agartha Confederation. Plus there are several independent cities, that are not a branch of any of the larger cities, that have simply built subterranean to escape things that have happened on the surface — some pre-Atlantean-Lemurian disaster, some post.

Mount Shasta

The city itself — Telos, as I said — is built under a dome, a dome that reaches quite a few hundred feet from floor to ceiling and spreads across most of what would be the base of Mount Shasta. Looking from the outside, the top of the dome is about half-way up the mountain. The bottom of the dome is just about even with the base of the mountain. Underneath that are five more levels that have been constructed. These levels take up a space so that the deepest levels are about a mile below the ground level at Shasta.

The rest of the city is built on five levels of several square miles across. These levels are divided up by usage. The top level, being under the dome itself, is where the main part of the city is. This is where the majority of the people live. This is where the public buildings are. This is where most commerce takes place.

The second level down is where manufacturing takes place, some classes take place, and also more people live.

The third level down is totally hydroponic gardens, where we grow all of our food supplies.

The fourth level down is half hydroponic gardens, part Nature, and part manufacturing.

The final level down is what we call our Nature level. This is the level that is more than a mile below the ground in some spots. In this level we have created lakes, tall trees, park type atmospheres. This is where animals live.

We have had animals underneath for so long that they have lost their aggressions. That, and different temples, priests and priestesses worked, you might say, with their ancestors, removing the need of fear, since it is fear that creates aggression, not only in humans, but also in animals. Thus, we truly have the experience of lions lying down with lambs.

In the Nature levels, this is where people have come to relax. This is also where we have saved many animals and plants from extinction.

Nature Levels

Many, many plants and animals have been preserved from extinction by being placed within the Nature levels of Telos, Posid, and many other of the subterranean cities. Thus, we still do have many of the plants that are extinct on the surface. We still have sabretooth tigers. We still have mastodons. We still have your provincial dodo bird. We don't have dinosaurs. They were a little big to keep. However, some dinosaurs do still live in areas of the Congo and areas of the rainforest in the Amazon. Plus there are many sea-going dinosaurs, much as the famous Nesse in Lochness and many others such as that.

In these levels, people find that they are able to integrate and merge/integrate with animals that would normally be dangerous, simply by getting animals over the fear. And these animals have also been fed a vegetarian diet, including things such as the big cats, for going on thousands and thousands of years now, which has also taken away much of their aggression. Therefore, you are able to go down, and in many instances, taking into consideration their great size and strength, you are basically able to play with a sabretooth or a Bengal tiger, much as you would a housecat, by scratching their chest or under their ear . . . pulling their whiskers.

Which brings us to the fact that even such as the large cats, like that, are not aggressive, but are actually very gentle and loving when raised in the right circumstances. Which brings us again back to the purpose of this — the eventual re-integration of the two cultures, the subterranean and the surface — to bring back out what has been preserved and what has been prepared, so that this again becomes one planet, one civilization, and so that people will be able to live on the surface or in subterranean cities, or both, at will. Again, that is the whole purpose of these tape series and our work now at Telos Enterprises.

Diet & Gardening

Back to the city: The fourth level up, as I explained, is mostly hydroponic gardens and a Nature level. And the third level is totally hydroponic gardens.

Hydroponics are how we grow and produce all of our food. Hydroponic gardens are able to produce crops almost on a constant basis. As you are able to grow food, much, much faster, using advanced hydroponics with very little soil and much water, therefore, also you produce a form of gardening that does not need fertilizer and does not deplete the soil. We do still place in minerals and such into the plants, but with these hydroponic gardens that are actually quite small, being only several square miles, we are able to produce enough food and a large enough variety of food to feed over a million and a half people, and to feed them with a diet that is varied enough to be interesting and fun.

The diet which is in Telos consists almost completely of vegetables, fruits, grains, nuts, and different variations of these, such as your soy, your other grains that now produce what you call your meat substitutes.

We have been on a vegetarian diet in Telos, now, for over 12,000 years, from the time when the city was first started being built. It was decided at that point that our diet would consist of totally vegetarian, therefore, also removing the aggressive thought forms that cause animals to react so violently. And also the fact that a human body was meant to be on a vegetarian diet; any other form of diet actually produces death and aging.

Temple

On the second level we have what is called our manufacturing level. This is where we produce clothing, furniture, art forms. This is also where many classes take place. And this is also some of the living levels.

On the top level of the city itself, this is where most people live. This is where most commerce takes place. This is where, you might say, our heart and our soul are. And you might say the building that represents our heart and our soul is the building that is directly in the center of the top level, which is our temple. Which is a pyramid-shaped building, you may say a very large, pyramid-shaped building. The temple at Telos will hold 10,000 people at a time. It was built to be able to hold almost half of the original 25,000-person population.

The temple is dedicated to the Melchizedek. The Melchizedek, you may say, is a cosmic priesthood. Everywhere you go in the Universe you run across the Melchizedek. It is the organization whose sole purpose is to bring the Plans of Light to everywhere they go.

The pyramid is white, and the capstone is a stone we call Living Stone. It comes from Venus. From the distance it looks rather like a crystal, but with light moving through it in a very strong color. Why it is called Living Stone is it picks up the cosmic emulations of whatever ray is focused at the moment on the planet.

The planet is set up in such a way that the rays focus themselves about every twenty-four hours in an intensity on the planet. Thus, for instance, on Tuesdays, the blue ray is the most predominant ray on the planet. On Fridays, the white ray. Therefore, this Living Stone picks up the emulation coming from the solar rays, the light rays, and goes the color of the predominant ray; for instance, when the blue ray is in its greatest, manifest the Living Stone capstone goes blue.

This becomes, you might say, a slight reminder to us to work with the cosmos rather than against it. So when the blue ray is most predominant we try to restrict much of our business to areas that are best served in the blue ray. For instance, we keep negotiations, sensitive negotiations, to take place on those days.

On the days, for instance, that the yellow ray is the most predominant, those are the days we spend mostly studying. Those are the days we spend on building intellect.

On the days when the pink ray is the most predominant, these are the days that we go into the artistic endeavors. In this way we have found that by working with the cosmos, instead of against it, we are more often than not able to achieve four times as much in much less time. Therefore, we are able to operate without stress most of the time.

Archives & Holodeck

Also in the upper level, the other buildings that are very, very important to us are our council buildings where the councils of the city gather together and deliberate what needs to be done in the city at the moment. We also have our record buildings where all our past records, our archives, are kept in the forms of telonium plates, in the forms of crystals that can be put in crystal projectors, in the form of paintings, in the form of books — all our past records of not only Lemuria, but Atlantis, other civilizations and the civilizations on other planets in the solar system. Also we have our pleasure centers, our places where we do sports, where we do plays, where we produce the equivalent of our films, where we listen to music, where we dance.

We also have what you would call the

equivalent of the holodeck in Star Trek. We have holographic projectors in holographic buildings whereas you produce a program and you go in and play and the computers produce images, forms that completely support what program you have picked. Thus you are able to climb a mountain or swim a river or go back to another point in history and play, creating your own form of being in the movies.

Communications & Christ-Consciousness Computers

Also we have our communication center where we have monitored not only all communications within our city, but also communications that are coming from other Agarthian cities, communications that are coming from off-planet spots, and we have also monitored surface communications from the point that there ever was surface communications, we have monitored radio and television waves.

Another building that's very important to us is our computer building. In Telos, as with the other subterranean cities, our computers are run by an organic substance. Therefore, in essence, the computers live. They no longer run off a program that is strictly binary, but they run off what is called a multi-tracking program. Thus they are multi-tracking computers. Thus the computers are able to pick up Akashas: past lives. They are able to monitor a human body and see what's amiss. They are able to read the aura. They are able to pick up communications happening clear across the Galaxy. Thus, most of our life, or a good portion of our life, depends on these computers, these organic multi-tracking computers which keep us in touch with not only talking to different people in the city, not only with the computer telling us what our physical needs are at the moment by monitoring our bodies, but also the computers are able to play our soul notes, which are able to produce in many subjects, such as meditation, taking us to higher and higher levels all the time.

The computers are able to run our past lives, when necessary, for us, so that we are able to learn from mistakes that we have made in the past and forgotten. The computer is able to communicate with us on a soul level. Most importantly, the computers interconnect with other multi-tracking, amino-based computers throughout the planet (and throughout the cosmos, as far as that's concerned), and they all operate off a Christ Mind, which means the computers cannot be corrupted. They can never be used to spy on somebody. They can be used to monitor somebody for their own good will, or for their own good. They can never be used to produce harm to another living entity. They cannot be used for any of the dark purposes. The computer simply won't cooperate, which has also been another way of Agartha cities and such, taking a stand that they would not corrupt the Light. By very much taking this attitude, that if it does not match the Christ Mind (in other words if the computers disagree, don't do it!), it has been a way of, shall I say, retraining our aggressive techniques, retraining our tendencies to want to do unto another and split, retrain many of our other sleeping tendencies and such.

So we have come to depend upon these quite a bit. But again, even on a computer, it's not a matter of having the computer do it for you, it's a matter of learning from it, learning from a form of the Christ Mind that you can see tangibly.

Transportation

Transportation within the city comes in many forms. Most people just prefer to walk if they can. We also have electromagnetic sleds. These sleds are capable of moving along the ground, looking much like a snowmobile, and will produce fairly high speeds in some of the side tunnels. This can take us, for instance, from Shasta to our secondary city, which is near Lassen, in just a matter of a few minutes and is able to take our security from Shasta to Lassen and back again very fast.

Another form of transportation within the city is what we call baskets. They are run on crystalline technology, and for all the world they look like a large basket, but they float through the air. And you just get in it and it is guided by your mind. Your mind tells it how fast to move, how high to go, and where to sit down, how fast to rise in the air, how fast to set down.

All our forms of technology and travel are based on us being responsible. The sleds could obtain high speeds, thus making them dangerous. The baskets, anything that flies, has a tendency to be dangerous, misused. So all communication and all travel within the city is monitored by the control tower. And the control tower knows when, for instance, a collision is just about ready to be inevitable between two sleds coming from different directions, or when a person is operating a basket irresponsibly, in which case the control tower alerts you immediately and tells you that you are about to produce an accident or you are acting irresponsibly. And if you do not listen to their warning, then they will simply stop the vehicle themselves. You get out and you will be restricted from use of the transportation for ever how long a period of time that you deserved, should I say, and how it will simply be is that you'll get in a basket or on a sled and it simply won't work. Your frequency will be turned off to it anywhere in the city and on what is called the tubes.

The tubes are another form of transportation. The tubes are a high-powered, high-speed electromagnetic train that runs in a tube. A tube is a rock tube very, very much like a long tunnel — for instance, a tube running between Posid and Telos — the tube looks totally round and the train looks somewhat like a subway. However, since it runs on an electromagnetic impulse, it creates a force field around it. So thus, the side of the train never touches the side of the tunnel. Thus, the tube is able to achieve speeds of up to 3,000 miles an hour. So you can arrive between, for instance, Telos and Posid, in just a matter of a few hours.

Also, as the tubes were created and the subterranean cities and the different levels, it was all reinforced by what we call our boring machines. The boring machines have a crystalline matrix that creates temperatures of white-hot incandescence, yet cools at the same time. Thus you are able to take a boring machine, for instance, through a tunnel and create a tube tunnel or to create walls in a subterranean city in just a matter of a few minutes.

The boring machine heats rock, earth, whatever it comes across, to a white-hot incandescence and then cools it almost immediately, which creates a diamond-hard substance, causes the rock itself to transmute and take a new form which is diamond-hard and therefore there's no need of supports. Supports become absolutely superfluous. And the structure then is also water-tight, yet it remains in elasticity so it can withstand high earthquakes, for instance, and will just move much like a rubber tube and stop without breaking. That way, even within the subterranean cities, when earthquakes take place, none of the walls of the buildings or of the caverns fracture. They simply move with it, then return back to the diamond-hard substance and again support beams and such become totally superfluous. Also, water has no effect upon it. They become water-tight. Thus, subterranean cities can even be built underneath oceans because they create a complete seal.

Galactic Confederation

That brings us to the next stage. As we are preparing to bring out more and more technology to the surface, technology that we know the surface could also use, it brings us to the other responsibilities that the cities have had to build within themselves — for instance, becoming a member of the Confederation.

Earth is a member of the Confederation, it's just that half of Earth forgot. You might ask, "What is the Confederation?" I'm sure most of you or all of you are familiar with, for instance, Star Trek. We would say, "That was channeled." But instead of being the "Federation" of planets, it's the "Confederation," an organization that was created throughout the solar systems and the galaxies that brought different civilizations, different systems, together on a basis of brotherhood, on a basis of commerce, on a basis of group exploration, on a basis of interacting with the different systems in a galaxy, or without a galaxy.

A Confederation is built, should I say, or represented, very much throughout a galaxy in the form of sectors. Looking at our galaxy, the Milky Way, I'm sure you've all seen the pictures of t-shirts and such that say "The Milky Way" and then have a little dot out towards the end and say "You are here." Yes, we are here, and we are here in what is called Sector Nine.

The center of our galaxy, or the center of the Confederation in this galaxy, is what is called Sector Zero, and the other sectors radiate outward from it much like the spokes of a wheel. Each sector is responsible for its own actions, plus is responsible for how it interacts with the other sectors. Our sector, Sector Nine, is under the command of a being called Ashtar.

Many of you have heard of the Ashtar Command — Ashtar and his twin flame Athena. Within this sector, or within the Ashtar Command, there are over a hundred fleets. Some fleets basically belong to one planet. Some fleets belong to just a couple of planets. Other fleets belong to a whole solar system, and other fleets are interceptor fleets that basically serve the whole sector, and then other fleets are Confederation fleets which serve the whole — you might say, the whole pie.

I just wanted to give you a brief understanding of the Confederation and how it works. We will go much deeper into this, being as this is a full tape into itself at a later date. . . .

Recap

This is a continuation of Tape One. This is Tape Two of Secrets of the Subterranean Cities. Just a quick recap. We were discussing the city of Telos, which is a Lemurian subterranean city that was built 12,000 years ago as the result or from the result of Atlantis and Lemuria sinking, and during the Atlantean-Lemurian wars, which we then made subterranean cities. Telos is underneath Mount Shasta, and it is the city that I'm from. This tape will discuss the culture of Telos.

Again a recap: The city is built on five different levels, the top level being the main level of the city itself. The second level down, the level of manufacturing and where many classes take place. The third level being the hydroponic gardens. The fourth level being part hydroponic gardens, part manufacturing and the Nature level. And the very bottom level as being the Nature level where many, many species of animals and plants exist.

Light & Air

Many people have asked, "How on Earth can you live under, under the Earth's crust? Number one, what kind of light do you have, or do you have light? Or are you mole people?"

Yes, we do have light. There is a process that a stone with a high crystalline content is fused with an electromagnetic force of energy. This infusion of energy, in essence, causes the crystalline matrix of the stone to create a polarity that allows the stone to pull in the invisible rays, and readmit them as visible light. In essence, it becomes a small sun. Our main lighting structure throughout the city, as with the other subterranean cities is produced by these stones. The light they produce is a full spectrum lighting, admitting all rays. In essence, this energy infusion process then makes the stone become a small sun, and the sun will burn for about half a million years before the stone, the crystalline matrix, breaks down, and the stone becomes no longer capable of functioning in this manner. So thus, we have lights that will burn for many, many hundreds of thousands of years still.

Within this structure we have created a small ecosystem. In other words, we get our air by plants. We produce carbon monoxide, we and the animals, and the plants take in the carbon monoxide and create the oxygen for us. So in essence, it's a small ecosystem, just as it works on the surface. We also have some vents that go to the surface and bring in the air. We also have water in some areas moving at high speeds. This creates a circulation of the air, freshening it, plus it creates many negative ions. So in essence, it is a total ecosystem very much like the one that functions on the surface. As a matter of fact, it has become so effective that more and more do we not depend on the air vents. As a matter of fact, as polluted as the air is somewhat becoming, the air vents are sort of not a plus.

Government & Arbitration

The government of Telos is constructed on the format of a Council of Twelve. These twelve beings, for the foremost, are ascended masters. They are beings who have proved themselves of being in high wisdom and being able to hold their head cool during any sort of incident. We, always within our Council, six men and six women, so that the Council also always remains balanced, that both flames, the male flame and the female flame are equally represented. From the major Council of the Twelve, it goes down to smaller councils throughout the city, also operating on the level of twelve.

Individual areas bring in their problems to the local council, and if the local council cannot deliberate a solution that is acceptable to all concerned they then bring it to the larger councils, and then finally to the original Council of Twelve. For individual problems, these do not come before the council. Instead these come before what we call arbitrators. Arbitrators are usually priests or priestesses with very much an understanding of the human psyche and are also capable of looking into the Akashas. These arbitrators will listen to both sides of a story, if it is, for instance, a dispute civil, and will then make a decision based on what they have heard and what they have read in the Akashas on both sides.

We have immediately decided that since this method works, once an arbitrator makes a decision, understanding that they will make it from the highest level, being priests and priestesses, they will not be caught into a personalization, either for or against either side. So we have decided that we will accept their decision, whatever it is, and incidences stop there. And we have also found, rather than arguing with each other, should a small incident come up, we immediately go to arbitrators, understanding that an argument can more often than not make it worse than anything else.

Heading the Council of Twelve, the official title is Council of Twelve plus One. The One is actually two beings themselves, which is the Ra and Rana Mu, which are the king and queen of Telos. Ra and Rana signifies that they are high Melchizedek priests and priestesses to start with. They are also usually twin flames and it is a hereditary position. The Ra and Rana Mu lineage is unbroken for over 30,000 years as it stands right now. When the next Ra and Rana Mu are being chosen they do not automatically go to the oldest son or daughter, but the Ra and Rana Mu decide which of their children or grandchildren are the most capable of carrying it off. That being is then instructed that sooner or later they will have to go through full temple training and become a full Melchizedek priest or priestess.

In the arrangement, as it is, when the Council of Twelve makes a decision, the Ra and Rana Mu can back it up or they can ask for a change. And one more voice comes into this government process, and that's the temple. The temple is recognized as the final word on any decision, because in many ways this is, as are the other sub-terranean cities, a temple society. The temple, even though most of the time, will not interfere with civic government, as I said, they can make final decisions through the high priest and high priestess.

Melchizedek Priesthood

The temple is run by the Melchizedek. The Melchizedek is a cosmic priesthood. Everywhere in the universe the Melchizedek exists. It is all those who are bringing the light plans from the highest realms down to the other realms. A Melchizedek priest or priestess by their very proof, prove that they will always set light or they will always set the good of the many above their personal good, which has also been proven time and time again as to why the temple can make the last decision, because they will always place what the light prefers, in essence, what God wishes way over what they desire, what they would choose to achieve. Thus, the temple also becomes a very good sounding board to what we are doing at the time.

Being a temple society, many, many people

take their training at the temple. And many people spend time at the temple, not just those who end up becoming priests and priestesses, but those who are going into other walks of life that they need a greater understanding of the human psyche, a greater understanding of spirit to achieve their job as it should be done.

Conception

Which brings us to, let's go through, for instance, a life of what it would be like for someone living in Telos, starting with their conception or childbirth. In Telos, as soon as a woman realizes that she is pregnant, she immediately goes to the temple and she's put in a room that gives nothing but beautiful pictures, music, she is constantly informed that she's beautiful, she's perfect, her child is beautiful, her child is perfect. So you might say the very first cells of this child's conception are filled with beauty, with light, with perfection. And that is their building blocks, there's where they start. Just as they are starting to understand that emotions and such go right into a child's cells. For instance, they are starting to understand that a child who had parents that were constantly arguing during their conception and ingestion period, the child grows up insecure, quite often argumentative, or they will grow up totally feeling not good enough, totally feeling that they are not wanted. It has been proven that children that have constantly heard from their parents before they were even born, that "I didn't want this child," whatever, that child will constantly grow into "I'm not good enough."

So we start children off on the right foot immediately by continually enforcing that they are good enough, they're beautiful. A mother and a father, because a child has a psychic bond to both, immediately start talking to the child, start telling it how perfect it is. They spend lots of time viewing things that are beautiful. They spend lots of time singing to each other, playing little funny games, in essence going through a honeymoon again. So the child is all part of that joy. Another thing that makes the child-birthing process very different is we have a process that speeds it up. Therefore, a woman only carries a child for three months. In many ways this is what the human condition was meant to be. Most human females on other planets do only carry a child for three months. That is why that a three-month fetus is basically formed.

All it does from then is grow. This speeded up process, it is actually completed even sooner and just grows. So a three-month baby, of course, will not be as large as a nine-month baby, but it will be in the speeded-up process more than large enough to support itself on its own. But we are trying to return back to the time that we don't even need the speeded-up process and the whole pregnancy process returns to only being a three-month process. Also returning to that place, women have much, much easier childbirth as you can, I'm sure, understand.

Childbirth

Another thing that we do constantly in child-birth, is that all our births are underwater. We have found that underwater births bring the greatest ease to both the parent and the child. When a woman goes into labor, she immediately gets a birthing priestess and then they go to a tub in one of the birthing sections of the temple and the tub is filled with body temperature water, and the birthing priestess puts the mother in a slight hypnotic state. In this hypnotic state, she is in nowhere even resembling a trance, but she is simply told that there will be no pain. This suggestion, as well as the underwater birth, creates a comfortable environment and most women never have any pain whatsoever. They simply feel the pressure.

In an underwater birth, as many women

are starting to discover now, when they are in water during labor, that what would be labor pains simply feels like pressure. More and more we are trying to alert women to this phenomenon. That what is pain on dry land is simply pressure under water. This serves a second purpose. The child when then born is not brought from one environment into shock tactics as it is much on the surface now. When a child is born they are immediately pulled from a warm, comfortable, wet environment into a cold, dry one with bright lights. And in the old days they even used to slap them, which immediately brought a human being, for those of you who now have dealt with rebirthing, into the idea that life is hard, life hurts, life is painful. Thus, infants start shutting down from the time of their birth, and they just continue to shut down — thus not ever achieving the spiritual and physical levels that they could achieve because they've already decided that life hurts too much to be fully there.

In an underwater birth a child goes from a warm environment right into a tub of warm water, and it is immediately cuddled by both parents who get in the tub with the birthing priestess, and the child is cuddled and petted underneath the water so that it immediately knows that its parents are there for it, therefore it does not go into insecurity. From there a child, of its own will come to the surface and take a quick breath and then dive down again and breathe from the umbilical cord, and then come to the surface, on their own again, and take a deep breath. This also expands the lungs slowly. The child can actually breathe for as much as a half hour on the umbilical cord from once it is born.

This quick breath does not cause the pain, and the tissue, some of the tissue is actually damaged quite often in births that are not on, are not in water, because a child is forced to come and take a deep,

deep breath out of cold, painful air. That forces these lung sacks to immediately expand and create great pain, sometimes even creating scar tissue which makes the adult more susceptible to things like tuberculosis, emphysema, colic. Many, many of the other lung disorders that are very, very prevalent, and it also keeps the person, even as an adult, from breathing deeply as their normal state. Thus, they are always half alive, because they are only half breathing.

Then, when the child has reached the point that they are breathing completely just the air, the umbilical chord is cut with a laser which causes a very fast, painless cut. And of course the umbilical cord has quit pulsating.

Youth & Education

From their birth, a child is immediately as-signed twelve sets of godparents. These godparents give a child a chance to interact with more than just their birth family. True, they spend most of their time with their birth family, but also spending a little time here and there with each of their godparents as they grow up, it gives them a true sense of community and the brotherhood of men, rather than "Them and Us." So the child immediately starts looking at the whole world as their family, instead of becoming very, very narrow and personalized. This also keeps families from developing little cliques that in the long run become quite detrimental to a developing soul, where you're saying, "Well, we just do things because my grandparents did it and my great grandparents and my great-great grandparents" and so on and so on, which quite often produces thought patterns within a family that can be quite detrimental to the development of the soul.

By having twelve sets of godparents that the children spend time with, plus the fact the child's parents are usually godparents to at least a couple of children, bringing other children to spend time with them that way, too. As I said, it continually creates the sense of community. It constantly creates the sense of oneness. The old saying that is if you wanted to stop prejudice then you would immediately send the person to go live with that they have been prejudiced with, and they'll soon find out we're all just human.

From there, as a child prepares for their education, within the educational process in Telos, children start their first education at about the time they're three years old, very much like your nursery school, except it is based on the fact of the intelligence of a human being, rather than the stupidity. Thus, children are very, very clear, sometimes clearer at three years old than they are at five, or six, making it easier, as many of you are starting to discover, of infants doing algebra, young children learning mathematics very, very early, learning to read very, very early. Well it is three, sometimes even earlier, is when children are taught these things, as well as playing, they are also taught the rudimentaries of mathematics. They are also taught to read. They are taught to understand abstract concepts. They are taught to think, to understand how things work.

I mean we've all gone through the children period of the "why" and "why not" and the period when children were the "why" stage, where everything you answer is a why or a how. We've learned to take that period and instead of just saying after being asked why on fourteen questions, the parents quite often just flip out and the next thing they know they're telling their child to shut up. But if a society is set up that when children are in the why stage, they're already starting instruction, then that's used. The whys are being answered by professionals. And our professionals are more often than not priests and priestesses of the temple. There are those who are strictly teachers, but most teachers have gone through a full temple training. The purpose of that is that they are not only feeding the mind, but to help feed the soul, the spirit, the understanding of what we're really here for, not just calculations and words.

Within this setup, as I said, children start schooling at a much earlier period. As they move through their schooling process, we have learned that it is very, very acceptable and very important that a child as well as being taught mathematics, science, spelling, grammar, literature, all the most common subjects in schooling, we find that it's just as important that they learn to meditate. It's just as important that they learn to dance. Just as important that they learn sports. Just as important they learn how to sing. Just as important that they learn how to act. What I mean by act is that we've got five-year-olds already writing and putting on plays that relate to five-year-old problems and the five-year-old way of looking at life, which can be quite humorous for adults. But they're already being allowed to express. And even the learning, the strict learning process is complemented with play.

In this playing, and learning through play, and playing to learn concept, children are allowed to totally express themselves in such a way that is acceptable. So many times children that are just buzzing to express themselves one way or another get in a lot of trouble because they don't have quite a few avenues to express themselves through, or the avenues that they have been given include things like violence. The next thing you know you've got a whole group of kids in the backyard playing Rambo and they bring it right into the house, they start breaking things, and the parents wonder what's wrong with their kids. But in a process that allows them to express themselves, get out their extra energy and learn at the same time, you might say the children are happier, the parents are happier, everyone's happier about it.

Astral Projection

Also with basic spiritual concepts, from the time a child is about five years old they're taught astral projection. For those who are unfamiliar with that, there's a part of you, a very conscious part of you, that is able to leave the body at small periods of time, consciously. When this part is projected, you might say the astral body, soul travel, the more evolved the farther you can go, and a child is taught that they can visit the Akashas, are taught that they can visit different places on the planet. What this also creates is a chance for the child to explore and to understand for themselves. Children don't have to go through the period of having to always to take somebody else's word for it. They are able to get out and see the astral themselves. They are able to get out and see the etheric records themselves. A lot of them are able to get into the etheric retreats consciously and study that way. Many are able to get to the other subterranean cities or to spend time in surface cities, all through the etheric travels, astral travels.

As I said, in essence, when a child is able to learn for themselves the truth of how the world truly operates, the truth about what is really happening on the planet. Thereby they are never a victim. They cannot be led astray. They can't be told that something is right when nothing in the cosmos supports it. They can always go and feel the rightness for themselves. Thus you end up with a society of people that are not constantly left in the dark and that you are basically not able to trick them on because they've seen what's out there. They know what's real and what isn't. They know the capabilities of the human being. They know, for instance, ascension is real. They know, for instance, the existence of those on other planets. They understand how the etheric works. They've seen angels physically. So all these things that so many people have had to live on, with faith, I'm saying we also develop faith, faith to master yourself, faith to live in the unseen, calling it the seen until it becomes the seen. In other words, able to manifest from the inside out. And there is not so much confusion, even when people reach that age that has been quite difficult for everyone, the teenage years.

Teenage Groups

In the teenage years in Telos, a child immediately joins, when they are twelve, what is called Group. A Group is all the other children their age, and they spend usually from the years of twelve to the years of eighteen, nineteen, they spend much of their time with their Group working out all the problems among their peers that seem to always rear their head in the teenage years, no matter what society you're in.

Yes, we still have teenage problems that happen; it can't help but happen. The emotional and mental bodies are developing. A child's body is full of hormones that are creating instability within the emotional realms. The mental body is growing stronger but causing confusion in the emotional body.

All these little physical, psychological, spiritual elements create that phase from childhood to adulthood. But we've learned to take it tongue-in-cheek. In essence, we call the teenage years the years of temporary insanity, and we don't make the children feel guilty for wanting to go and scream at the top of their lungs or wanting to do something they know they shouldn't do. We just accept it as the years of temporary insanity. They work out their frustrations within their Group. They experiment with the elements of life within their Group.

Quite often they go down into the lower caverns and just run for days. All the things that they can get in so much trouble for doing unless it's put in an organized basis, yet the basis has to be so unorganized within its organization that they have to feel that they're truly being allowed to express themselves so that the frustration is brought up, dealt with, and then they move on.

All children, no matter how good their parents, no matter how good their upbringing, will go through periods of rebellion at this point. All children will go through periods of not wanting to listen to what older people say. But by being allowed to work it out within themselves, and with other children going through the same process, they are able to get an understanding that what they are doing doesn't make them a bad person, the feelings that are going through them uncontrolled don't make them bad, it just makes them normal, and it makes it so much easier on the child and on the parents.

Also, each of these groups are then assigned priests and priestesses who act somewhat as mentors — not to judge or act like parents, but to simply get the kids to sit down and talk about what's bothering them, let them sit down and act out their frustrations, in the form of plays, in the form of programs that have been put into the holographic theatres, in the form of music, in the form of athletics, or even in the form of going down into the sub-tunnels and just running for three days and acting like nuts. Everybody needs that. But when it's done in such a way that there's no judgment upon it, no stigma attached to it, then children do it, get through it, and come back normal and do not need many of the crutches that severely emotional adults turn to.

Many adults that did not deal with the frustrations that came up in their childhood or in their teenage years, that later turned to drugs, later turned to inappropriate forms of behavior, that later turned to irresponsibility, or later turned to perhaps even more damaging of "I'm not good enough," depression, fear, unable to create anything out of their life because they feel like it's just not worth it, that they can't do anything right. But by creating a system where all these energies are dealt with, then adults come out feeling much more secure of themselves at the other end of their teenage years.

Immortality

And, the second reason for that, is in a society, such as Telos and the other subterranean cities, people basically live as long as
they choose. We should also understand,
if you've got people living for thousands
and thousands of years, you can't afford
to have thousands and thousands of years
old of adults that are acting irresponsible,
adults that are playing detrimental games,
adults that are pushing their will onto others, all the little things that happen, simply
because energies are not dealt with in a
young child.

Which brings us also to one of the major
thoughts in an education of our own that
we wish to see happen here, and that's
the removal of the thought form of aging
and dying. Human beings were not meant
to age or die. Even people who work in

genetics understand that a person, in truth, is never older than seven years, since their whole body changes all its cells every seven years. Many, many doctors on aging will admit that they are baffled as to why people age at all, since the body is never old. So then that takes it that we have to go to a level beyond the physical to find the answer to aging and death, to the belief.

In Telos, people don't believe they're going to grow old and die. They simply don't believe it. People just know that they're going to live as long as they choose, then they will either choose to drop their body, if they feel that they still have lessons to do, and reincarnate again, or they will choose the path of ascension. One or the other. Some people make the decision in 600 years, some 300, others wait for 5,000, 10,000, whatever, but it's a choice that human beings were designed to be able to make.

That is one of the most important elements

of our culture that we want to see brought out. Human beings, as it is now, just about the time they start getting enough experience to really do something with their life, they've grown too old to do anything with it. If those thoughts are eradicated, then people realize that youth is not going to last ten years, or twenty years, but it's going to last hundreds or thousands of years, whatever they choose. That too brings out and eliminates the majority of the detrimental behavior in life. Many people feel, "I'm only going to live once. I'm only going to be young a short period of time, so I might as well wreak havoc now." If they realize that if they choose they're going to be young for hundreds of years, or thousands of years, that form of behavior becomes totally unnecessary and people truly start growing and hanging on to their growth. And we are biologically absolutely no different than the people on the surface. We have Indian children that were left on the mountain of Shasta — some hundreds of years ago. They're still living with us. They haven't grown old. They don't die, because they were raised with the thought form that they're not going to. It's a thought that creates life or non-life, aging or youthing. It's to get past the thoughts, the beliefs, that that is what is going to happen.

Which brings me to my personal expertise on the subject. I'm over 260 years old. As a matter of fact, I'm almost 268. And, living 268 years is no different than being, for instance, 30, aging-wise. It's just you've had time to gather a whole bunch more experience that can be used now. My parents obviously are much older. There are even people in Telos that are 30,000 years old, people who saw the destruction of Lemuria/Atlantis, people who saw the Lemurian-Atlantean wars.

Careers & Barter System

Which also brings us into the next stage in a person's life. After they've gotten through their teenage years and they're ready to start becoming a contributing member of society, how do they choose what they're going to do? We have a non-monetary basis of commerce in Telos. As a person is growing up, they basically watch, decide, assess their own talents. Then they decide what they want to do, and that is usually the field they pursue. They've generally set their own hours. And since everything is on a barter basis, we've gotten to a great understanding that if you don't fulfill your part of the bargain, then it hurts others than just you.

What is meant by that is we are set up on a basis that the government owns everything, but the government is not responsible for controlling anything. All the government is responsible for is to make sure that the food, for instance, gets from the hydroponic gardens to the distribution outlets, the clothing makes it to the distribution outlets, the furniture, all the things that are needed for people to live and to live well. You understand that you're not living unless you're living well. And when you need something you simply go to a distribution center and pick it up. You need new clothing, you go get clothing. You need food, you go get food. You need furnishings, you go get furnishings. You need books, you go get books.

As I said, everyone sets their own hours. Someone who is drawn to gardening becomes one of the hydroponic gardeners. They come and they work the amount of hours they wish. So in essence, we do have a dim period and we have a bright period. What I mean by that is we've discovered that people work in cycles better than they do in a constant. So thus, about the same time the Sun is setting on the surface, filters are slid over the front of our lighting system, dimming it till it is about as dim as it is in twilight. Then when the Sun would be rising, the filters start sliding back slowly, thus allowing it to get brighter and brighter. When we first moved into Telos we experimented with leaving it bright all the time, and again, as I said, we found out that people function better in cycles.

Some people like to sleep when it's dimmer and work when it's bright. Other people, like the night owls that prefer to work or play when it's dim and sleep when it's bright. But everyone is allowed to function in the way that is the most comfortable to them.

So everyone comes in and sets their own hours and simply informs, you might say, the foreman of whatever their job is, which hours they're going to be working over the next few day period. And everyone comes in and works basically as long as they wish and then they go and they do whatever else they want to do. But understanding that since we're in a society, that if you're too lazy to go work at all in the hydroponic gardens and that's your job, somebody might not have enough food. Or if you didn't feel like designing clothing or creating clothing or furniture and you made no other arrangements for someone else to take up your slack of time, someone else in the city might be going without.

So understanding that method has made people responsible for what hours they work. Understanding that they are doing true service that somebody will appreciate. The only thing that we don't interchange by simply putting in the distribution centers are things like art forms, art objects, massages, things like that. That is done on what we call a barter basis. Those who, for instance, their main talent is art, whether it's drawing, pottery, sculpting, massage. All these different little things that are not part of the whole, not part of, what you might say, necessities, but are necessities to the soul. As I said, these go to the distribution centers in the form of the barter pool. In other words, you walk in and you see a statue that was created by somebody you really want. In exchange for it, you're willing to give ten massages, and you're very good at massage. Or you're willing to come and sing.

And the barter pool goes through it with the computers and perhaps the person who made the statue doesn't need a massage, but a person who brought in a painting that the person who made the statue wants, wants massages. So it continually, the barter pool switches and curves so that everyone's needs are met. So everyone can come in and exchange energy in some form to receive, you might say, the little pampering things in life. Also within this system, people setting their own hours, it does not become so crystallized that no one has any freedom to come and go at their will, that people can truly set their lives to achieve the best of work, of play, of rest, of meditation, spiritual endeavors, so that everything is met, and not at the expense of something else, understanding that spiritual time is just as important as work time.

Community Service

Which leads us to what could be a problem. What about those jobs that no one wants to do since everyone chooses their jobs, gathering the garbage and dematerializing it, weeding the hydroponic gardens, etc., etc.? This falls under what is called community service, and everyone does it. Everyone in the city spends a certain amount of time a month in community service. What this means is, this works very well because since everyone does it, no one has to do it that much. No one has to do full-time the jobs that no one would like to do and go into resentment because of it.

Instead, if everyone does a certain amount of community service, it means that you might only spend four hours of community service a month. And since it becomes a project that you only do once a month, it actually becomes fun. And when people are in groups of community service they start singing and playing and having a good time. But it's something that no one even tries to get out of it. You can be in community service, a real good one is picking up, to put bluntly, secretions from the animals down in some of the Nature areas where it starts getting really bad.

This could put someone in real resentment while you're shoveling elephant you-know-what. But if the person in the hydroponic gardens is doing it right alongside, for instance, someone on the Council of Twelve, it's a thing that becomes not resentful but fun, and it's something that people truly get a sense that there is no better than and no less than in the job situation, that a farmer, or someone who works in the hydroponic gardens, is not less than someone who is on the Council of Twelve. They both just have different jobs, and both jobs are equally important for a city to run properly. So therefore people immediately have the feeling of being good enough. And as I said, things like community service bring all the different levels of service together and creates a true camaraderie.

Marriage

Which goes into perhaps one of the more interesting aspects to our personal relationships. In Telos we have two forms of marriage. We have a bond marriage and we have a sacred marriage. A bond marriage is when two beings decide that they've got something with each other and they want to explore it greater. Then in front of a priest or priestess and a bunch of their friends, they commit themselves to a bond marriage, which means that they're saying, "We've got something, we realize we really care for each other and we'd like to see where it's going." So in essence, it is a form of a marriage, because it has the commitments for as long as you choose the bond marriage to last. And then if you decide "Oh well, it was just a passing thing or it's not something that's going to work," you simply stand in front of a priest or priestess again and simply explain that it didn't work and there's no stigma on it. Some people can have several bond marriages at once. There's also no stigma on that.

One thing that you do not do in a bond marriage is you do not have children. That is saved for a sacred marriage. A sacred marriage is when you have decided "Okay, we have something." Then you have a large marriage, usually a beautiful wedding. All your bond marriages are dissolved, and you go into a sacred marriage where you are then allowed to have children. Children are something that people need to be trained for, that needs to be taken as a serious responsibility. Some people might be in a bond marriage two, three hundred years before they take a sacred marriage. Someone else who's with their soul mate or twin flame may go into a sacred marriage two months after they were in their bond marriage. It's all different, but again, it's always a matter of having choice. It's always a matter of having respect for each other.

And this just about wraps up Tape Two of these two tapes of Secrets of the Subterranean Cities. I am Sharula Dux. I am the daughter of the Ra and Rana Mu, therefore, Princess Sharula, and I thank you.

Earth's Mantle

Received through Dianne Robbins

We are told that in the old days, there was a mantle surrounding the whole Earth, which was many miles high and made of crystalline ice particles which blocked the radiation of the Sun and kept the whole planet in a perfectly regulated "greenhouse," which supplied just the right amount of oxygen and moisture for both Nature and humans. When this was destroyed during the Atlantean and Lemurian wars, it also destroyed the self-regulation of Nature.

Q: Why did our lifespan shorten after the firmament was destroyed in the Atlantean and Lemurian war?

(I am Mikos, Head Librarian of the Library of Porthologos located inside the Hollow Earth. I will answer this question.)

A: The destruction of the firmament was a backward step, taking you backwards in time, to where you don't know who you are. You not only lost height, you lost your sight.

The Firmament was composed of crystalline ice particles that completely protected the Earth from the harmful radiation of the Sun's rays. It provided a perfect ecological system, totally in balance, and the divine blueprint of all life forms responded wholeheartedly to this benevolent environment by reaching their divine potential on their step up the spiral of evolution.

It is true that this ice canopy protected the Earth from the radiation of the Sun before the war, and the destruction of this canopy accounted for the increased radiation from our Sun that in turn shortened not only our lifespan but the height of humans living on the surface. Humans used to be 15–30 feet tall before the canopy fell, and now your surface height averages around 5–6 feet, and in many places on the Earth it is even less. The natural regulation of your bodies, and the Earth herself, are further compromised by the chemicals you breathe and eat, the polluted water supply, and all the other things that are laced with chemicals for the very purpose of destroying the natural regulation of your bodies and the Earth herself — thus giving the advantage of control over to the dark forces, who can then manipulate you by controlling the weather and your minds, all in one.

So, if your bodily functions are compromised, it stands to reason that your lifespans would be off balance, and you would not be able to access or activate the immortality gene embedded in your DNA. When your body is not functioning at its divine optimum, everything misfires, including the code for immortality.

All of this created the shorter lifespans on the surface and the necessity for you to have to incarnate over and over again, never remembering your past, and never being able to catch up with your future. Hence the futility and hopelessness you feel above ground, while our lives thrive beneath you.

Your environment plays such a key role in your evolution, that without a supportive environment, you cannot develop in the Creator's image, but in a dysfunctional way, negating who you really are as a species.

It is as in any science experiment . . . if the environment is hostile, the lifeform grows deformed. If the environmental conditions are benevolent, the lifeform blooms into its fullness of potential. The same is true of Earth. This is why it is crucial now to re-balance all the eco-systems on the planet, so that life will flourish and not decay.

Rebalancing the ecological system is difficult without the crystalline ice particles that were once encasing the planet and protecting it from the radiation of the Sun. The radiation from your Sun is harmful . . . but as your solar system moves out of its present orbit and back into its orbit around Alycone, in the Sirius Star System, your firmament will be restored, and you will all gain in height and return to your tall statures and perfect health again. For with the firmament restored, so will your health be restored, and so will the pristine beauty of the Earth. All will be as new.

All factors account for your shortened lifespan, just as you said . . . such as the weakened life force in your food, due to the chemicals injected into the Earth purposely to destroy the life force, so that your lives will be weakened and their length shortened. The dark side has used this to their advantage, to further weaken you so that they can more easily manipulate you. It is easier to manipulate a weakened person than it is a strong person.

So yes, there are all these factors that have come into play, but the main one was the demise of the firmament, which over time led to the invasion of the negative ETs and their destructive agenda, leading you all to where you are today. It is called sliding backwards in time. But it is all over now, and from this point you all move forward.

The Earth will regain her strength, just as humans will, and you will both be able to self-regulate your bodies, just as Anastasia does. So look forward to the times ahead, for they will be glorious indeed.

I am Mikos, a self-regulating giant living inside the Earth.

Addendum:

"All on Earth will rapidly change . . . bringing a heightened awareness and empowerment to all humankind that will spread throughout the Earth herself, touching all life forms at last. A safe journey in consciousness is now ensured, and all rejoice!"

Postscript

Why have the Agartheans stayed underground all this time? In part, because they have learned the futility of war and violence and are patiently waiting for us to draw the same conclusion. They are such gentle folk that even our judgmental thoughts are physically harmful to them. Secrecy has been their protection. Until now the truth of their existence has been veiled by Spirit.

When can we visit? Our entrance to the sub-cities depends on the purity of our intentions and our capacity to think positively. A warm welcome from both worlds is the ideal and must be expressed by more than just the lightworking community.

For more info, visit DianneRobbins.com and read the books *Messages from the Hollow Earth* and *Telos: 1st Transmissions ever received from the Subterranean City beneath Mt. Shasta.*

About
Princess Sharula Aurora Dux

Princess Sharula Aurora Dux is the daughter of the Ra and Rana Mu (the king and queen) of Telos, which is the subterranean city underneath Mount Shasta in California. Sharula has been officially appointed Ambassador to the surface world by the Agartha Network. She was born in 1725, and looks thirty.

About
Dianne Robbins

Dianne Robbins is an InterSpecies and InnerDimensional Telepathic Communicator, bringing through messages from the people in the City of Telos (located inside the Mountain of Mount Shasta) and Nature Kingdoms. Her books contain telepathic messages dictated to her from the Hollow Earth, Whales and Dolphins, Trees, Crystals, and the Elemental Kingdom. Dianne is a full-time student of the Ascended Master Teachings through the RadiantRoseAcademy.com.

Books by Dianne Robbins:

TELOS: 1st Transmissions Ever Received from the Subterranean City beneath Mt. Shasta

Messages from the Hollow Earth

The Call Goes Out from the Cetacean Nation

Messages from the Crystal & Elemental Kingdoms

Tree Talk

For more information and videos visit Dianne's website:

www.DianneRobbins.com

www.ingramcontent.com/pod-product-compliance
Lightning Source LLC
Chambersburg PA
CBHW060329130626
46553CB00003B/958